my first puzzles

Fun with Words

Helene Hovanec

Illustrated by Ed Shems

Sterling Publishing Co., Inc.
New York

10 9 8 7 6 5 4 3 2 1

Published by Sterling Publishing Co., Inc.
387 Park Avenue South, New York, NY 10016
© 2006 by Helene Hovanec
Illustrations © 2006 by Ed Shems
Distributed in Canada by Sterling Publishing
c/o Canadian Manda Group, 165 Dufferin Street,
Toronto, Ontario, Canada M6K 3H6
Distributed in the United Kingdom by GMC Distribution Services
Castle Place, 166 High Street, Lewes, East Sussex, England BN7 1XU
Distributed in Australia by Capricorn Link (Australia) Pty. Ltd.
P.O. Box 704, Windsor, NSW 2756, Australia

Sterling ISBN-13: 978-1-4027-4820-2
        ISBN-10: 1-4027-4820-5

INTRODUCTION

When EASY FIRST PUZZLES was published in August 2005, I found out, to my delight, that adults were eager to purchase puzzle books for the young solvers in their lives. They seemed to believe, as I do, that "It's never too early to start solving puzzles." FUN WITH WORDS is the second book in this series for three- and four-year-olds. All the puzzles are meant to be solved by a child and adult working together. It's okay for the child to direct the adult as he/she writes in the book!

ADULTS:

If you're a puzzle lover, you enjoy giving your brain a mental workout with all different types of puzzles. Now you can pass along this love to a significant child in your life.

CHILDREN:

An important adult in your life bought this book for you so you can have lots of fun at the same time that you're learning so many new things.

So, grab a pencil and start solving. Then check the answers at the end of the book. Enjoy this time with your parent, grandparent, aunt, uncle, cousin, teacher, friend, sister, brother, or other important person in your life.

Helene Hovanec

Hi There

Circle the two chalkboards that have
the word **Hello** written just like this.

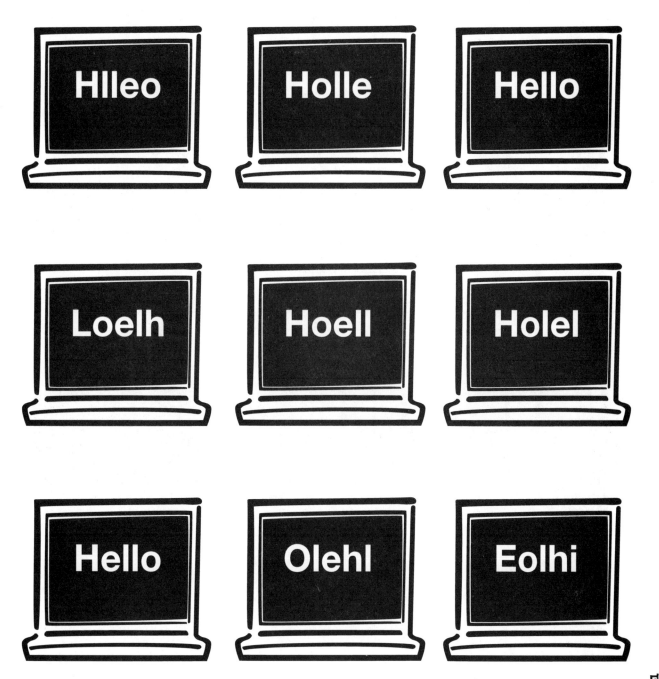

All Alone

Each line in the box has one letter that is different from the others.
Circle that letter. Then write it in the correct space below.
Do the same thing for each line and you will find a kind of flower.

1	H	H	T	H	H
2	U	O	O	O	O
3	E	E	E	L	E
4	A	I	A	A	A
5	R	R	R	R	P

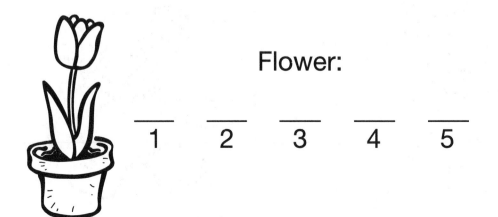

Flower:

___ ___ ___ ___ ___
1   2   3   4   5

6

"Beary" Nice

Draw a line between the teddy bear on the left side and its "twin" on the right side. When you are done you will have three sets of "twins."

Picture Crossword 1

Name each picture. Then write the word into the grid.
Be sure to check if the word should be written Across or Down.

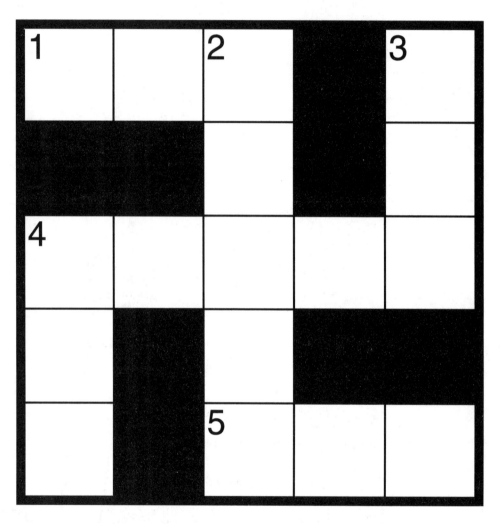

Across

1   4   5

Down

2   3   4

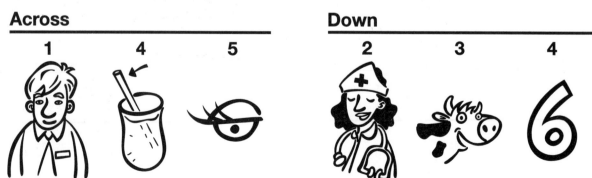

Dog Walk

Help the dog get to his leash by taking the correct path from the top to the bottom of the picture.

So Symbol 1

Circle each letter with this symbol ✳ in front of it.
Then read only the circled letters to find the first two lines
of a famous rhyme. Can you say the rest of the rhyme?

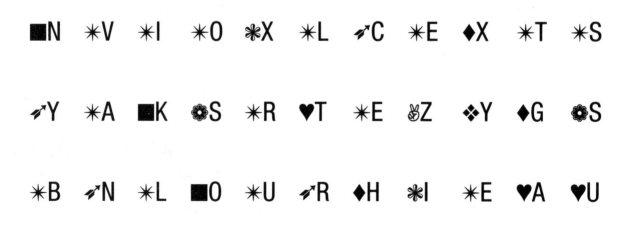

◆P ✳R ❖A ✳O ✿A ✳S ✳E ✌L ✳S ◆T ✌W

◆M ✌W ✳A ♥I ✳R ◆L ✿O ❖Q ♥U ✳E ❖G

✌M ✳R ■H ➶F ♥U ✳E ❖G ✳D ♥B ✳Z ✳X

_____

■N ✳V ✳I ✳O ✳X ✳L ➶C ✳E ◆X ✳T ✳S

➶Y ✳A ■K ✿S ✳R ♥T ✳E ✌Z ❖Y ◆G ✿S

✳B ➶N ✳L ■O ✳U ➶R ◆H ✳I ✳E ♥A ♥U

_____

Family Find

The names of six family members are on this list. Each one is also hidden in the box below. Look at each line to find the name of a family member. Then circle it. After you have found all the words you might want to name all the people in your family.

AUNT

BROTHER

COUSIN

FATHER

MOTHER

SISTER

Y	M	O	T	H	E	R	D
C	O	U	S	I	N	B	L
G	H	F	A	T	H	E	R
J	S	I	S	T	E	R	M
B	R	O	T	H	E	R	V
Z	Q	N	M	A	U	N	T

Clothes Call

There is one piece of clothing on this page
that is not on the opposite page.
Which one is it?

Fooling Around

Connect the dots from 1 to 20 to find a funny person.

Travel Directions

Pick one letter and follow the line connected to it until you end up at one of the road signs. Then write that letter on the sign. Do this six more times to find the name of a place to visit in your hometown. The letter "H" has been placed for you.

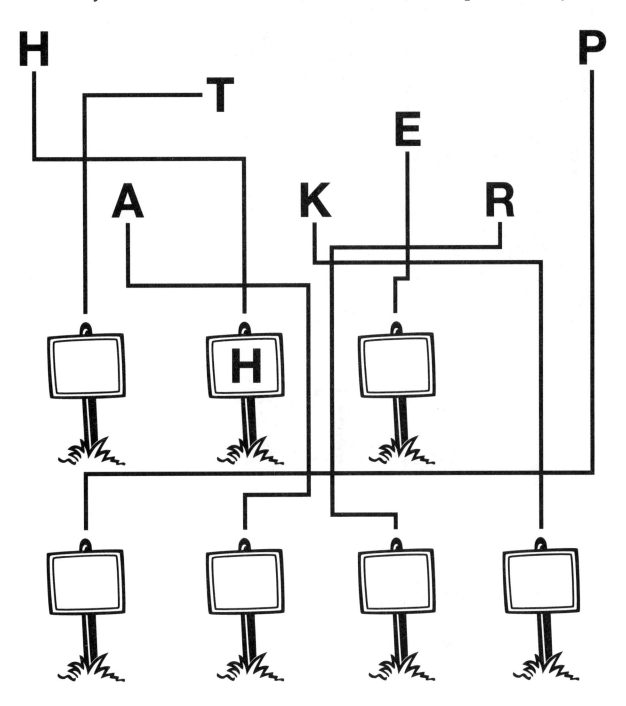

Halloween Costumes

Each Halloween costume will fit into one spot in the grid.
Look at the letters that are already in the grid and use them to
help you put each costume into its spot. Hint: Start with the G
and find the only costume that begins with that letter.
Write it in the grid, going across. One word will lead to
another word until the whole grid is filled in.

GHOST

PIRATE

PRINCESS

SKELETON

WITCH

16

Hats Off

Each person on this page
lost the hat he or she was wearing.
Draw a line between
the person and his or her hat.

Not the Same

Circle the five things in the picture on the opposite page that are different from the picture on this page.

Moving Letters

Follow the directions below and you will find the first part of a nursery rhyme. Do you know the rest of the rhyme?

Write the letter A into spaces 18 and 22

Write the letter E into spaces 6, 15, and 27

Write the letter F into spaces 13, 14, 25, and 26

Write the letter I into spaces 2 and 8

Write the letter L into spaces 1 and 5

Write the letter M in spaces 7 and 11

Write the letter N in space 21

Write the letter O in space 20

Write the letter S in spaces 9, 10, and 17

Write the letter T in spaces 3, 4, 16, 19, 23, and 28

Write the letter U in spaces 12 and 24

$\overline{}$ $\overline{}$ $\overline{}$ $\overline{}$ $\overline{}$ $\overline{}$ $\overline{}$ $\overline{}$ $\overline{}$ $\overline{}$ $\overline{}$ $\overline{}$ $\overline{}$ $\overline{}$ $\overline{}$ $\overline{}$

1 2 3 4 5 6   7 8 9 10   11 12 13 14 15 16

$\overline{}$ $\overline{}$ $\overline{}$ $\overline{}$ $\overline{}$ $\overline{}$ $\overline{}$ $\overline{}$ $\overline{}$ $\overline{}$ $\overline{}$ $\overline{}$

17 18 19   20 21   22   23 24 25 26 27 28

Now do the same thing again to find the first part of a different nursery rhyme. Do you know this rhyme?

Write the letter A in spaces 13 and 15

Write the letter C in space 8

Write the letter D in spaces 3 and 23

Write the letter E in spaces 11 and 17

Write the letter G in space 7

Write the letter I in space 5

Write the letter K in space 4

Write the letter L in spaces 2, 10, 22, and 27

Write the letter M in space 16

Write the letter N in space 6

Write the letter O in spaces 1, 9, 21, and 25

Write the letter R in spaces 18 and 19

Write the letter S in spaces 14 and 24

Write the letter U in space 26

Write the letter W in space 12

Write the letter Y in space 20

$\overline{}$ $\overline{}$ $\overline{}$ $\overline{}$ $\overline{}$ $\overline{}$ $\overline{}$ $\overline{}$ $\overline{}$ $\overline{}$ $\overline{}$ $\overline{}$ $\overline{}$ $\overline{}$
1 2 3   4 5 6 7   8 9 10 11   12 13 14

$\overline{}$ $\overline{}$ $\overline{}$ $\overline{}$ $\overline{}$ $\overline{}$ $\overline{}$ $\overline{}$ $\overline{}$ $\overline{}$ $\overline{}$ $\overline{}$ $\overline{}$
15   16 17 18 19 20   21 22 23   24 25 26 27

Name the Food

Name each picture and write its first letter on the blank space. Then read the numbers from 1 to 8 to spell out a popular lunchtime food.

1. _____

2. _____

3. _____

4. _____

5. _____

6. _____

7. _____

8. _____

Do the same thing again to find another food.

1. _____

2. _____

3. _____

4. _____

5. _____

6. _____

7. _____

8. _____

Almost the Same

Draw a line from a word in the first column to the word in
the second column that means almost the same thing.
We did one for you.

DADDY	GLAD
HAPPY	MOTHER
LOUD	LEAVE
MOMMY	SPEEDY
GO	TOUCH
FAST	GIFT
PRESENT	FATHER
FEEL	NOISY

Animal Sounds

Draw a line from the animal on the left side
to the sound it makes on the right side.
We did one for you.

ANIMALS

SOUNDS

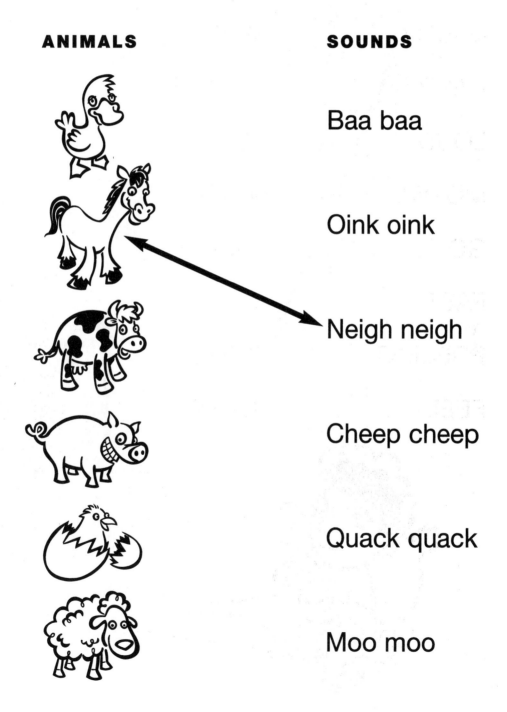

Baa baa

Oink oink

Neigh neigh

Cheep cheep

Quack quack

Moo moo

Rhyme Time

Each picture on this page rhymes with one thing on the opposite page. Can you say all the rhymes?

Code Fun

The letters in a name were replaced by symbols.
Look at the box to figure out what letter each symbol stands for.
Then write that letter on the blank space above the symbol.
Read the words to find the name of a nursery rhyme character.

⊖ = E	★ = H	✳ = I	■ = N
♥ = O	✿ = S	♠ = T	✂ = W

___ ___ ___ ___

✿   ■   ♥   ✂

___ ___ ___ ___ ___

✂   ★   ✳   ♠   ⊖

Color Match-Up

Draw a line between the color word on the left side and the color word on the right side that is exactly the same.

YELLOW	RED
BLUE	BLACK
GREEN	WHITE
BLACK	ORANGE
WHITE	BLUE
RED	BROWN
ORANGE	YELLOW
BROWN	GREEN

Green Things

Each green thing will fit into one spot in the grid. Look at the letters that are already in the grid and use them to help you put each word in its spot. Hint: Start with the D and find the only word that begins with D. Write it in the grid, going down. One word will lead to another until the whole grid is filled in.

DOLLAR

GRAPE

LETTUCE

LIME

PARROT

PEAR

TURTLE

30

Find the Flags

Five flags are hidden here.
Can you find and circle each one?

Add-a-Letter

On each line, look at the three-letter word in the first column.
Then look at the four-letter word in the second column.
The letters in both words are the same EXCEPT that one extra
letter has been added. Write the extra letter in the blank space.
When you are finished, read DOWN the column
to find something to eat for breakfast.

3-letter word	4-letter word	Extra letter
EAR	PEAR	_____
NET	NEAT	_____
BAD	BAND	_____
ART	CART	_____
WAY	AWAY	_____
PIN	PINK	_____
HAT	HEAT	_____
TOP	STOP	_____

Do the same thing again to find something
else to eat for breakfast.

3-letter word	4-letter word	Extra letter
CAP	CAMP	_____
FOR	FOUR	_____
OLD	FOLD	_____
LET	LEFT	_____
RAN	RAIN	_____
WET	WENT	_____
FAT	FAST	_____

Cross-Outs

Follow the cross-out directions for the letters in the grid.
When you are done there will be some letters
on each line that were not crossed out.
Read them to find the names of five things
you might play with.

CROSS OUT:

1 D   1 F   1 H   2 N's   1 Q   3 V's   1 X   1 Z

H	B	L	O	C	K	S
P	U	Z	Z	L	E	F
N	N	Q	B	A	L	L
G	A	M	E	V	V	V
D	X	C	L	A	Y	Z

Housing Market

Each creature in the left column has its own special "house" in the right column. Match the creatures and their "houses" by drawing lines between them.

Book Time

Circle the two books that have the same titles.

1 HIS BOOK

2 MY BOOK

3 HER BOOK

4 YOUR BOOK

5 MY BOOK

6 OUR BOOK

Now circle the one book that isn't the same as the others.

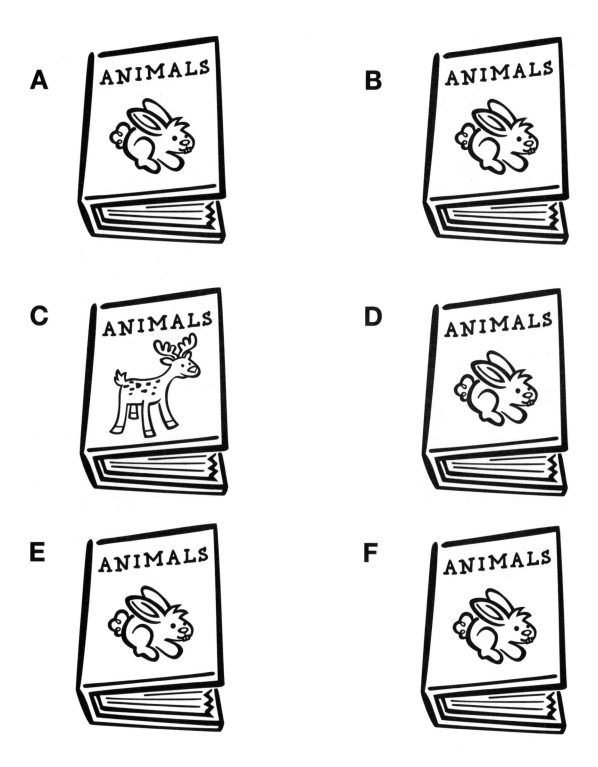

A ANIMALS

B ANIMALS

C ANIMALS

D ANIMALS

E ANIMALS

F ANIMALS

Odd One Out

Cross off the one word in each group that doesn't belong with the others.

1.

NUMBERS

FIVE

SIX

SEVEN

EASTER

2.

ROOMS IN A HOUSE

KITCHEN

PARK

BEDROOM

DINING ROOM

3.

ZOO ANIMALS

DESK

ELEPHANT

LION

TIGER

4.

COLORS

RED

BLUE

PIZZA

WHITE

5.

MUSICAL INSTRUMENTS

DRUM

FROG

PIANO

GUITAR

6.

DESSERTS

ICE CREAM

PUDDING

CRIB

PIE

7.
MEALS
BREAKFAST

LUNCH

GOLF

DINNER

8.
COLD DRINKS
SODA

MILK

JUICE

BELT

9.
THINGS TO WEAR ON YOUR FEET
SHOES

HAMBURGERS

SNEAKERS

BOOTS

10.
THINGS AT A BIRTHDAY PARTY
CAKE

CANDLES

GIFTS

THUNDER

11.
THINGS FOR WRITING OR DRAWING
PENCIL

TRICYCLE

PEN

CRAYON

12.
BABY ANIMALS
PUPPY

OCEAN

KITTEN

LAMB

Go-Togethers

Each picture in the left column can be put into something in the right column. Draw a line between the things that go together.

Picture Crossword 2

Name each picture. Then write the word into the grid. Be sure to check to see if the word should be written Across or Down.

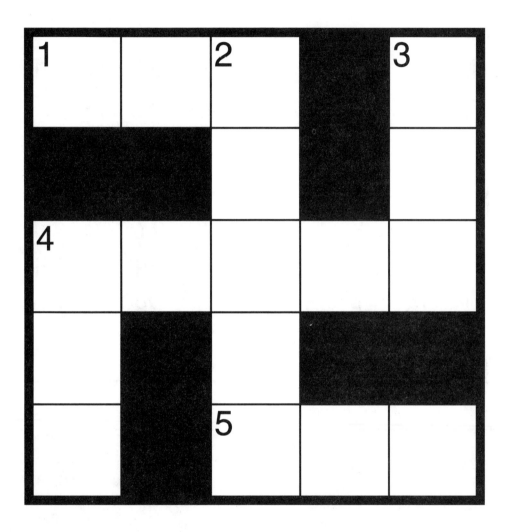

Across

1   4   5

Down

2   3   4

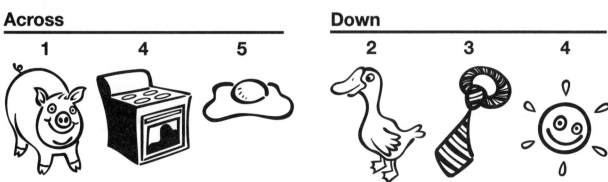

Checkout Lines

Circle each letter that has a check mark in front of it. Then read the circled letters to spell out the name of a fruit on each line.

1.	*M	√P	#I	√E	=L	@V	√A	&S	√R	!T
2.	√G	&D	√R	%C	@L	√A	#U	√P	(H	√E
3.	√P	+E	&A	√L	:B	√U	%E	@J	√M	=U
4.	√B	#W	√A	√N	?L	√A	=O	√N	&M	√A
5.	√A	!R	√P	$T	%V	√P	}Y	√L	=Q	√E
6.	√C	@N	√H	√E	?A	&G	√R	$S	√R	√Y
7.	+K	√B	=E	√E	%B	√R	√R	*Z	√Y	=D
8.	√O	=E	√R	+W	√A	*Q	√N	*P	√G	√E

1. _____

2. _____

3. _____

4. _____

5. _____

6. _____

7. _____

8. _____

Just the Opposite

Draw a line from a word in the first column to the word in the second column that is its opposite. We did one for you.

LEFT	BAD
GOOD	DAY
FAST	RIGHT
NIGHT	FULL
HAPPY	LAST
EMPTY	SLOW
FIRST	OLD
YOUNG	SAD

Location, Location

Follow the directions to find seven letters in the grid.
After you find a letter be sure to write it in the blank space on
each line. Then read down to find an outdoor activity.

FIND THE LETTER:

That is below the **+** _____

That is above the ***** _____

That is next to the **=** _____

That is below the **?** _____

That is next to the **$** _____

That is next to the **#** _____

That is above the **&** _____

?	+	R	A
P	C	G	*
=	M	&	W
#	N	I	$

Something's Wrong

There are five things wrong with this picture.
Can you find and circle all of them?

T-Time

Color in every box that has a **T** in it.
Then say the answer word two times and you will find
the noise made by the object on this page.

T	T	T	A	T	D	T	C	T	T	T	D	T	T	T
T	E	L	J	T	H	T	W	T	N	T	G	T	Q	T
T	F	I	V	T	T	T	K	T	O	T	P	T	X	T
T	S	D	U	T	L	T	R	T	A	T	Z	T	Y	T
T	T	T	C	T	M	T	B	T	T	T	Y	T	T	T

46

Track It Down

Connect the numbers from 1 to 20 to find
something that runs on tracks.

What Will It Be?

Each word in the box starts with BE. Read the sentences and choose one of the words to go into the blank space so each sentence is correct. Cross off each word as you use it.

BEANS	BEARD	BEDROOM	BEE
BELOW	BELT	BENCH	BEND

1. A bumble_____ is an insect that buzzes and makes honey.

2. You wear a _____ to hold up your pants.

3. If you get tired at the park you can sit on a _____ .

4. Green _____ are popular veggies.

5. Can you _____ over and touch your toes?

6. The hair growing on a man's face is called a _____ .

7. The opposite of above is _____ .

8. The place where you sleep is the _____ .

48

X It

Circle every letter that is NOT the letter "X."
Then read the circled letters to find a number word on each line.

1.	X	X	F	X	X	O	X	U	X	R	X	X
2.	S	X	X	E	V	X	X	E	X	X	X	N
3.	X	X	X	N	X	X	I	X	X	N	X	E
4.	T	X	X	H	X	X	R	X	E	X	E	X
5.	X	X	X	O	X	X	X	N	X	X	X	E

1. _____

2. _____

3. _____

4. _____

5. _____

49

Subtract-a-Letter

On each line, look at the four-letter word in the first column. Then look at the three-letter word in the second column. The letters in both words are the same EXCEPT that there is one letter missing from the word in the second column. Write the missing letter in the blank space. When you are finished, read DOWN the third column to find things you see at birthday parties.

4-Letter Word	3-Letter Word	Missing Letter
CLAP	LAP	_____
READ	RED	_____
NEAR	EAR	_____
CARD	CAR	_____
LAND	AND	_____
HEAT	HAT	_____
SHOP	HOP	_____

Do the same thing again to find more items
that can be found at birthday parties.

4-Letter Word	3-Letter Word	Missing Letter
BEAR	EAR	_____
COAT	COT	_____
SLIP	SIP	_____
PLAY	PAY	_____
OPEN	PEN	_____
BOAT	BAT	_____
NONE	ONE	_____
PAST	PAT	_____

What Is It?

Color in each box that has a **?** in it
and you will find a house pet.

?	?	?	*	?	?	?	+	?	?	?
?	#	@	!	?	(	?	*	-	?	&
?	^	$	{	?	?	?	%	)	?	/
?	^	%	$	?	#	?	=	+	?	>
?	?	?	@	?	(	?	!	*	?	=

Winter Fun

Help the sledders find their way to the bottom of the hill by taking the correct path from the top to the bottom of the picture.

Summer Fun

Connect the dots from 1 to 25 to find out what
the children are doing at the beach.

Doubles

On each line below, cross out the letters that appear two times. Then read the leftover letters to find five things you could see at the beach.

1 R R P V V A K K I L

2 M M S H O Y Y V E L

3 B D D L A N K G G E T

4 W A H H J J T E M M R

5 S E E A R R N P P D

So Symbol 2

Circle each letter with this symbol ✱ in front of it. Then read the circled letters to find the first part of a famous nursery rhyme.

□M   *T   ☆S   *H   *R   ◉J   *E   ☆A   ✳X   *E   ◉L

☆U   *L   ◉W   *I   *T   ◆K   *T   ❄C   *L   ☆Y   *E

*K   ❄V   *I   ☆R   *T   ❖I   *T   *E   ✱P   *N   *S

✣F   *L   ☆G   *O   ◆E   *S   ☆N   ✩E   *T   ✣Z   ✩R

*T   ✣A   *H   ◆O   *E   ◉G   *I   ❖P   *R   ☆P   ◉L

*M   ☆U   *I   ❖W   *T   *T   ◉X   *E   *N   ☆H   *S

Eye Cue Test

Look carefully at the objects on each line and
circle the one that is not the same as the others.

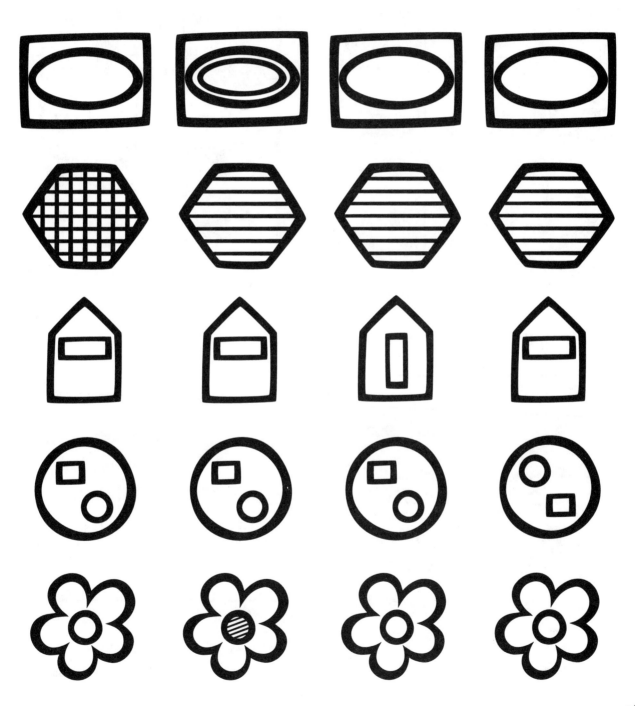

Answers

HI THERE
page 5

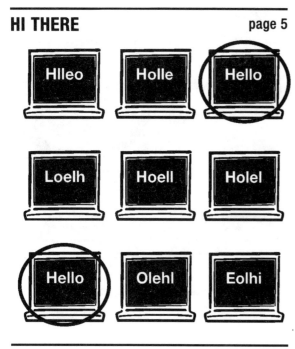

ALL ALONE
page 6

Flower: **TULIP**

"BEARY" NICE
page 7

PICTURE CROSSWORD 1
page 8

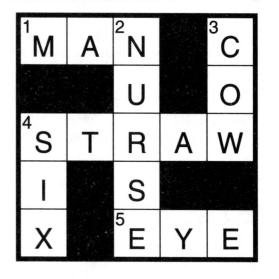

DOG WALK
page 9

SO SYMBOL 1
page 10

Roses are red, Violets are blue

The rest of the rhyme goes like this:
Sugar is sweet, And so are you

FAMILY FIND

page 11

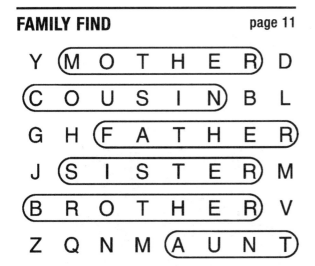

HALLOWEEN COSTUMES

page 16

CLOTHES CALL

page 12-13

HATS OFF

page 17

FOOLING AROUND

page 14

NOT THE SAME

page 18-19

TRAVEL DIRECTIONS

page 15

The park

MOVING LETTERS page 20-21

Little Miss Muffet sat on a tuffet

Old King Cole was a merry old soul

NAME THE FOOD page 22-23

1. **S**oap
2. **A**pple
3. **N**et
4. **D**og
5. **W**agon
6. **I**ron
7. **C**omb
8. **H**ammer

Food: **SANDWICH**

1. **M**ilk
2. **A**rm
3. **C**loud
4. **A**pron
5. **R**abbit
6. **O**nion
7. **N**est
8. **I**ce cream

Food: **MACARONI**

ALMOST THE SAME page 24

Daddy—Father
Happy—Glad
Loud—Noisy
Mommy—Mother
Go—Leave
Fast—Speedy
Present—Gift
Feel—Touch

ANIMAL SOUNDS page 25

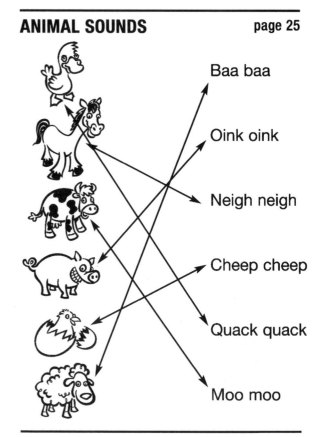

Baa baa

Oink oink

Neigh neigh

Cheep cheep

Quack quack

Moo moo

RHYME TIME page 26-27

Bed—Sled   Stamp—Lamp
Nose—Hose   Duck—Truck
Spoon—Moon   Cake—Snake
Bell—Shell

CODE FUN page 28

Snow White

COLOR MATCH-UP page 29

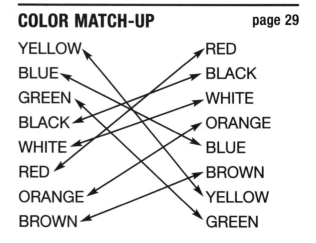

YELLOW   RED
BLUE   BLACK
GREEN   WHITE
BLACK   ORANGE
WHITE   BLUE
RED   BROWN
ORANGE   YELLOW
BROWN   GREEN

GREEN THINGS

page 30

FIND THE FLAGS

page 31

ADD-A-LETTER

page 32-33

3-letter word	4-letter word	Extra letter
EAR	PEAR	P
NET	NEAT	A
BAD	BAND	N
ART	CART	C
WAY	AWAY	A
PIN	PINK	K
HAT	HEAT	E
TOP	STOP	S

Answer: **PANCAKES**

3-letter word	4-letter word	Extra Letter
CAP	CAMP	M
FOR	FOUR	U
OLD	FOLD	F
LET	LEFT	F
RAN	RAIN	I
WET	WENT	N
FAT	FAST	S

Answer: **MUFFINS**

CROSS-OUTS

page 34

HOUSING MARKET page 35

BOOK TIME page 36-37

2 and 5 have the same title
C is different

ODD ONE OUT page 38-39

1. Easter
2. Park
3. Desk
4. Pizza
5. Frog
6. Crib
7. Golf
8. Belt
9. Hamburgers
10. Thunder
11. Tricycle
12. Ocean

GO-TOGETHERS page 40

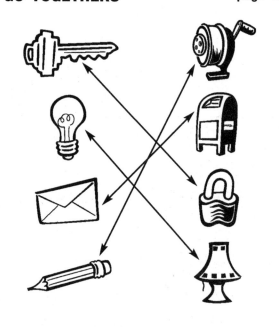

PICTURE CROSSWORD 2 page 41

CHECKOUT LINES page 42

1. Pear
2. Grape
3. Plum
4. Banana
5. Apple
6. Cherry
7. Berry
8. Orange

JUST THE OPPOSITE
page 43

Left—Right   Happy—Sad
Good—Bad   Empty—Full
Fast—Slow   First—Last
Night—Day   Young—Old

LOCATION, LOCATION
page 44

Camping

SOMETHING'S WRONG
page 45

T-TIME
page 46

The word is **CHOO**.

Say it two times: **CHOO CHOO**

TRACK IT DOWN
page 47

WHAT WILL IT BE?
page 48

1. Bee   5. Bend
2. Belt   6. Beard
3. Bench   7. Below
4. Beans   8. Bedroom

X IT
page 49

1. Four   4. Three
2. Seven   5. One
3. Nine

SUBTRACT-A-LETTER
page 50

4-letter word	3-letter word	Missing letter
CLAP	LAP	C
READ	RED	A
NEAR	EAR	N
CARD	CAR	D
LAND	AND	L
HEAT	HAT	E
SHOP	HOP	S

Answer: **CANDLES**

SUBTRACT-A-LETTER
page 51

4-letter word	3-letter word	Missing letter
BEAR	EAR	B
COAT	COT	A
SLIP	SIP	L
PLAY	PAY	L
OPEN	PEN	O
BOAT	BAT	O
NONE	ONE	N
PAST	PAT	S

Answer: **BALLOONS**

WHAT IS IT?
page 52

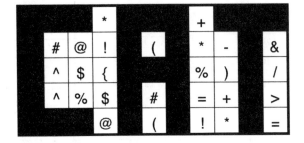

The house pet is a CAT.

WINTER FUN
page 53

SUMMER FUN
page 54

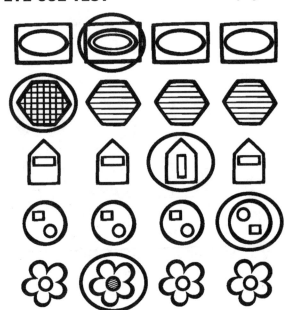

DOUBLES
page 55

1. Pail   3. Blanket   5. Sand
2. Shovel   4. Water

SO SYMBOL 2
page 56

Three little kittens lost their mittens.

EYE CUE TEST
page 57